BOA
EDITIONS LTD

T0161047

Birth Marks

BIRTH MARKS

Poems by
JIM DANIELS

AMERICAN POETS CONTINUUM SERIES, NO. 139

BOA EDITIONS, LTD. ❦ ROCHESTER, NY ❦ 2013

First Edition
13 14 15 16 7 6 5 4 3 2 1

For information about permission to reuse any material from this book please contact The
Permissions Company at www.permissionscompany.com or e-mail permdude@eclipse.
net.

Publications by BOA Editions, Ltd.—a not-for-profit corporation
under section 501 (c) (3) of the United States Internal Revenue
Code—are made possible with funds from a variety of sources,
including public funds from the New York State Council on the
Arts, a state agency; the Literature Program of the National En-
dowment for the Arts; the County of Monroe, NY; the Lannan
Foundation for support of the Lannan Translations Selection Se-
ries; the Mary S. Mulligan Charitable Trust; the Rochester Area
Community Foundation; the Arts & Cultural Council for Greater
Rochester; the Steeple-Jack Fund; the Ames-Amzalak Memorial Trust in memory of Henry
Ames, Semon Amzalak and Dan Amzalak; and contributions from many individuals na-
tionwide. See Colophon on page 112 for special individual acknowledgments.

ART WORKS.
arts.gov

State of the Arts

NYSCA

Cover Design: Sandy Knight
Cover Art: Jae Ruberto
Interior Design and Composition: Richard Foerster
Manufacturing: McNaughton & Gunn
BOA Logo: Mirko

Library of Congress Cataloging-in-Publication Data

Daniels, Jim, 1956–
[Poems. Selections]
Birth marks : poems / by Jim Daniels. — First edition.
    pages ; cm.
ISBN 978-1-938160-16-5 (pbκ) -- ISBN 978-1-938160-17-2 (ebooκ)
I. Title.
PS3554.A5635B53 2013
811'.54—dc23
                        2013013134

BOA Editions, Ltd.
250 North Goodman Street, Suite 306
Rochester, NY 14607
www.boaeditions.org
A. Poulin, Jr., Founder (1938–1996)

Contents

Poetica No Apologia Arte Kumbaya

I am not a minister's son or a former pro boxer
but I have a few things to say.

My children collect pieces of gravel
separating distinct piles of subtle color.

The Arbor Day Foundation sent me a dozen saplings
to plant anywhere in America. One night they landed

in an old lover's yard. Years ago.
I cannot tell you how many are still growing.

I know a woman whose life revolves around dried flowers
and that's okay. I never tire of the soft moans of mourning

doves, though some call them glorified pigeons.
What's wrong with pigeons, glorified or not?

As long as they don't shit on your head.
There's no predicting when you'll find a tiny shell

in a pile of gravel. So tiny you can almost imagine
an ant holding it to its ear and hearing the sea.

1. MegaEverything

Birth Marks

She was stymied by pizza, but not
by ice cream. She ordered vanilla
for its sound. She reigned as Queen
of the Isle of *You Decide*.

He had the patience of a splinter
working its way to the surface
and the business sense
of a herd of cattle.

She used her checkbook
to prop up every minor purchase.
He used cash for the benefit
of its traceless disappearance.

In short, he was a bad magician
and she the nervous assistant,
a match manufactured in a damp swamp.

Yet they set off enough sparks
to produce me out of a hat,
dazed by their applause.

Technically, I can't remember
that far back, but I can make up
a few things, given the lack
of memory and receipts.

MegaEverything

Generals gathered in their masses
Just like witches at black masses
Evil minds that plot destruction
Sorcerer of death's construction
     "War Pigs," Black Sabbath

The kid with stringy, blond hair
and torn Megadeth t-shirt
plagiarized song lyrics in his poem.
Black Sabbath? I said.
In my tiny gray office, he idly kicked
the metal desk, not meeting
my eyes. But then, he never did.

◙

1972, Michigan State Fairgrounds.
Black Sabbath ripped through the sharp
muffle of "Paranoid" on the distant stage
while I guzzled malt liquor from quart bottles
on a gloomy Saturday afternoon.

Ozzy stalking onstage scared me
in a familiar Detroit way—like a biker gang
crashing a high school party. I shook
it off. I raised my fist.

◙

He said turning in the lyrics was a test
but would go no further. Had I passed?
Those lyrics, the only semi-coherent thing
he'd turned in all term.

He could've fooled me with Megadeth lyrics.
Perhaps he had. We agreed that he should
drop. He hesitated at the door
like there might be one more thing.

◻

Sixteen. My ears buzzed
with dark-star feedback—
barking dogs, bloody teeth, fragments
of a thorough ass-kicking.

Ozzy's wire-cutter rasp asked
what happened when we died
and where, exactly, was the soul?
When a thunderstorm arced down on us,
no one fled. We stood and took it.

◻

Poetry was all I had that wasn't toxic.
I should've been easier on the kid.
His name was Chris. He slumped away,
black boots clomping against the floor,
and I never saw him again.

◻

The bitter mascara of the unrepentant
and the flawed jewel of self-absorption.
Ozzy's damaged now, beyond coherence.
He hadn't yet bitten the head
off a bat when I saw him in '72.

He only had to do it once. The rest of us,
Chris, we think about it every day
under the black, incoherent moon.

I Dreamt I Wrote a Poem About Jazz

I wrote *Miles, Bird, Trane*. I almost wrote *Dizzy*,
then I started thinking about Dizzy Dean,
the last 30-game winner in the N. L., 1934.
Denny McLain went 31-6 for Detroit in '68.
I was there when he won his 30th. Dizzy on hand
to offer congratulations. Young Reggie Jackson—
already the straw that tainted the drink—hit two homers
for the A's that day. What was he stirring? A martini?
A time bomb? In '68, when the wind blew in
off the river, Detroit still reeked wet smoke from the riots.
We'd taken the bus downtown for ladies/retirees day—
50 cents for kids under 12, so we scrunched
down with our shit-eating grins
for the ticket seller behind bars who didn't give
a shit, just wanted bribes for the good seats.
Somewhere in the city, Iggy Pop tried out lyrics
to "I Wanna Be Your Dog" and somewhere
Aretha cleared her throat and somewhere the MC5
turned it up another notch. After the game, we waited
on the wrong side of the street for the bus home
as the sun vamoosed, Billy Bowen clutching the two-ton ham
he won in the lucky number scorebook drawing.
Some young black men joined us, and Billy just
handed over the ham because our pastor
had been mugged outside the stadium last year,
but one guy said *Keep your damn ham, white boy!*
and we got on a bus that only took us further from home.
Denny McLain's in jail for the second time—raiding
the pension fund of his own company. Denny drank
a case of Pepsi every day. He had one more good season,
then spontaneously combusted. Like Detroit in '67. One match,
and nobody to blow out the candle. When his brother Paul
pitched a no-hitter in game two of a double-header
back in the '30s, Dizzy said *If I'd a knowed Paul*

was gonna throw a no-hitter I woulda throwed one too—
I mean Dizzy Gillespie. But all I know about jazz
could fit into one of Dizzy's cheeks. Those cheeks
were the size of pregnant grapefruit, but still. If I'd a knowed.
Dizzy Dean, Southern boy. Before Jackie Robinson landed
and his spikes caught in the dirt, and held.
I always drank my liquor straight and paid the price for it
directly. I haven't had a shot in eighteen years, and even that,
a reluctant toast. I can't pretend to like jazz. Iggy's music
mixed in the pounding din of car factories. We are all Stooges.
I wanna be your dog. Your frog. Your fog. Your wart hog.
No one will ever win 30 games again and so what? Is the ham
still riding around Detroit on a slashed bus seat
duct-tape silver over green vinyl? Nah.
James Brown repeats "I" nine times in a row
on "Please, Please, Please." "Riot," an easy word to make
from "Detroit." It was all about how you articulated "I"
in 1967. In 1968. In 1979, the singer Eddie Jefferson
gunned down "gangland style" outside Baker's
Keyboard Lounge, *the* place to hear jazz in Detroit.
If I'd a knowed, I'd a throwed. I'm back in line at the turnstile
outside the abandoned stadium, 2008. *But they built*
a new one! They built a new one! everybody says
like that's some kind of wonderful. And don't get me started
on the casinos. Dizzy. Miles/Bird/Trane. Am I validated now?
Am I authentic? Do I get to keep the ham? The autographed ball?
Free tickets to the next inappropriate comment?
I didn't live in Detroit. I lived in Warren. My Molotov
cocktail was a dud, but I went to jail for it anyway.
It's hard to punch yourself as hard as Adam Jenson did
in 1978 when he had that bad acid trip
and guzzling a fifth of whiskey wouldn't knock
him out. He didn't die! Exclamation point!
I'm going to change my name to Billy Ocean.
I'm going to get tough and get going.
I used to count things obsessively, but I stopped.
Somewhere a car door slams. It's the sound

of a drum set crashing. I want to like jazz!
But I don't! We all got our ways of spitting
out the chaos. I'm going to change my name
to Jayandee and get arrested for rapping backward
and upside down and crossing Eight Mile into Detroit
in my Emperor's Clothes. I'm buried in nostalgia
for Little Stevie Wonder. Blinded by the light
of his pure joy. I want to be Little Jimmy Daniels.
A little shame goes a long way to stir the drink.
So when black Willie Horton scored
the winning run and Denny McLain hugged him,
we could believe for 3.4 seconds that the city wasn't
going to burn down again. It's never stopped
burning. The underground salt mines of fiery tears distilled.
We were speed not heroin. We stood, destroying our hearing,
and refused to dance. Thus, I conclude. Thus, I make
the sign of the cross even though I don't believe:
Miles, Trane, Bird, Dizzy.

The Religious Significance of the Super Ball

The Super Ball was invented in 1965. Thrown down, it could leap over a three-story building . . . and would bounce on for about a minute after being dropped from a short distance. Wham-O's oft-repeated claim was that the ball had 92 percent resiliency.

My brother and I drank in the kitchen while the adults drank
in the basement. We'd lifted a twelve-pack from the fridge.

No one noticed or cared. Someone called to offer condolences
and I laughed till beer spewed out my nose.

What was funny about my grandmother dying?
She'd lived with us for fifteen years. We should've been . . . What?

Drinking with our parents instead? Her children, reunited members
of the unacknowledged "A" team of alcohol. Ten more years

and two more funerals before anyone tacked on the other A.

◻

My grandmother only drank Drambuie, and only for medicinal
purposes. Downstairs, they passed a bottle in her memory.

A young cousin's pocket bulged with a Super Ball.
They'd just come out, replacing the Slinky in Fadville.

We took the kid outside into the March thaw. *Grandma farts a lot*,
he said. He didn't live with her. He thought she still might be

coming back. We held him down and dislodged it
from his sticky hands. We hammered his Super Ball

against the street bearded with dirty snow
and watched it disappear.

◘

That chubby little cousin killed himself twenty years later.
Too much dessert. Eat your vegetables, dude,

I should've said. It bounced high and wild, ricocheting
off the parked cars of the grieving. Cold enough

for runny noses and the back of a sleeve. A good burn in the lungs.
Nobody wore coats. Nobody had any dope. Big bust

in the neighborhood. We lost the damn ball—kid started bawling.
We drove off in grandma's car—an old brown Buick with no radio—

to the five and dime and bought a bunch of Super Balls
with stolen cash from the funeral kitty. The kid was happy.

Everybody was happy. A Super Ball orgy. My brother and I
stood at each end of the block, firing them back and forth,

watching them rise over our boxy little houses till it got dark
or we ran out of beer or got cold or somebody barked us back

into the wake to move the ping-pong table or drive Aunt Millie home.

◘

It's okay to laugh. Aunt Millie'd caught us. *Cool, Aunt Millie—
did you ever get high? Got any dope?*

Grandma liked The Irish Rovers. I was taking requests,
cranking up "Danny Boy" at 45 rpm till it almost rocked.

We bought grandma a new rosary each year.
Blessed by the Pope. Kissed by the kids in Guadalupe.

Made by blind dwarves in Omaha. We'd each inherited one.
They jiggled in our pockets like Chiclets, the cross

a crotch discomfort. I don't know how grandma
would've wanted to go out, but not as Farting Grandma.

Where'd everybody go? Just me and my brother
at the kitchen table, into the Drambuie ourselves,

sick with memory.

▣

I'd loved her, little old grandma, but I was
a Stupor Ball. Jesus was her Super Ball.

I shouldn't have been driving her old car.
The moon came out to shame me.

Fifteen years of her shrinking, reduced
resiliency, curling into herself with the fragile

delicacy of a charcoal snake till she disintegrated
and blew away. So, get mad, get drunk, laugh loud.

Drinking as hobby, sport, part-time job. As she went deaf,
silence leaked from her bones. She must've believed

she was returning to Jesus, bead by bead.
Nobody had any funny stories to tell about her.

Watching Super Balls erupt off cement
in a reckless, indestructible surge, I became addicted too,

and shame on me. 92% resiliency. I wound up
and smashed my grief into concrete, but it simply rose,

and rose, high, higher still.

Final/Not Final

Another student attempt. Horizontal?
Vertical? How deep? What if Western Psych
wasn't down the block? When I called, she said,
"Want to talk to Mark? He's here, too,"
the invisible ink of his mid-term disappearance
suddenly surfacing in my grade book.

She returned for our writing awards with neatly taped
wrists and her mother from Allentown
who claimed that her own flaming orange hair
had nearly caused a riot when she was nineteen.
Students either swarmed her or stared
from a distance. Her looks still stunning,
though her skin had paled into blank white paper.

So, who was stylishly fucking her before choosing
to return to his wife? Would her profs give her
incompletes? Or A's? We gave her our "newcomer"
award. I broke protocol to hug her, open space
blooming awkward between our arms, the cool gap
of her future. She transferred out of state.

◙

If your roommate commits suicide
you don't get all A's
though that rumor holds water
across the years. The water stagnates—
algae and grief and who gives a damn
when the fire alarms go off for real.
Mixing metaphors is allowed, and eating
with your fingers, and relentless laps
in the indoor pool. Lowercase
texting is allowed. Even ☺'s.

If your roommate commits suicide
you are not placed in witness protection
and given a one-way ticket anywhere
in the continental United States or Canada.
If your roommate commits suicide
you get a new roommate.

◘

When your magazine subscription expires,
they send you notice after notice. You know
how they send you one that says "Last Chance"?
Then another one that says "Last Chance"?

Those who succeeded.
Those who failed.
Those who kind of tried it
but let everyone know first.
Those who thought about it.
Those who wrote about it.
Those who never mentioned a word
then did it. Disappeared forever
onto the island of misfit teenagers
disappeared into opaque limbo land
disappeared into ice sculptures
and shrunken heads. Disappeared
into the Land of Empty Desks.

◘

Carbon monoxide or pills or wrists.
Few shooters. Wrist-slitters usually survive. Some
hang themselves. Though that too
is frequently botched. The pure impulse
of bridge-jumping, convenient and foolproof—
three killer spans over the nearby hollow.

◙

Teeth slam against each other.
Shadows erect their cold scaffolding, threatening
permanence. Life Geometry's untraceable
angles, the inability or unwillingness to reach a point
and turn, carry on. The lesson for today
is survival. The world's metal detector
failed us again. The thermometer
exploded with inaccuracy.
The lesson for today is
no more fooling around.

The Laying on of Hands

Their bodies touch, casual in the classroom,
fingers brushing thighs under cluttered desks.
Go home and fuck, I'd tell them

if I was high or not in charge. Lust oozes above
my low bark stripping somebody's words naked.
Their bodies touch in the casual classroom

of nodding heads half-detached, glazing out
into the gray February blah blah blah.
Go home and fuck! I'd tell them

if we were friends. A statue of our founder imposes itself
above dirty snow like twisted black coal, an effigy of me.
Their caustic bodies touch in the classroom. They know

each other. Everything. The floor burns beneath them.
My notes erupt in flames. I taste the ash.
Go home. Fuck you! I'd like to tell them.

It's not on the syllabus. I'm talking about character today.
Punctuation leads me astray. The boy the girl the ink bleeds.
Their bodies touch. Causality in the classroom.
Go home. Fuck, what can I tell them?

Approaching and Passing an Epiphany

On the turnpike I follow an old pickup
full of loose clutter and human mystery and think,
hey, I'd like to hop in the back and go with whoever's
driving this claptrap ramshackle vehicle and help them
unload this stuff on whatever planet they're crash-landing on:
O—no H, that old hark-and-hither kind of O—
O stained mattress and two bald tires and one rusty wheel
and an ironing board and a Big Wheel and a stuffed dog
and a paint-by-numbers kit and a "Whole Lotta Love"
by Led Zeppelin and an acoustic prayer book
and a young Elvis who means business
and a stack of cassette tapes recording the last words
of somebody's grandpa either having a stroke or drunk on his ass
and a green bowling ball and a vase shaped into the likeness
of a local stripper and forty-seven candles in various
stages of melted decrepitude and a monkey wrench
and a dog alive and barking and a rubber-banded deck of cards
consisting of seventeen aces and one jack of hearts and a stack
of *Reader's Digest*s with dog-eared joke pages
and a neatly rubber-banded bundle of envelopes
from creditors they are escaping and a bicycle once run over
by perhaps this very truck and a dozen plastic milk jugs
filled with green and brown liquids
and a pile of flapping clothes spilled across the bed
held down by plastic free weights from Sears
somebody going to get in shape some day
but the wind's having its say, so who knows
what they've lost already? They're dawdling. I switch
lanes, pass them up, watch them disappear behind me.
I make a little noise like *humph* or *ungh*,
but offer no pronouncements. I check
my gas gauge, odometer, make estimates
like an actuary and shrug at my own estimates
and question the reliability of the narrator

who might at any moment light a match,
set the whole damn thing on fire.

The Dark Miracle

Chimayó is home of the Santuario de Nuestro Señor de Esquipulas. Local residents walk miles, often barefoot, to visit. . . . Many take away "tierra bendita" (holy dirt) from a hole in the floor, claiming miraculous healings.

She handed me a baggie of holy dirt—
a gift from my new friend. Back at the motel,
reminded of various drugs I'd ingested
in various ways, I wondered if airport security

would sniff it out the next day. That night
in a curtainless room, I watched darkness
swallow the random lights of Albuquerque
while the freeway whoosh faded to a nearly

inaudible hiss. I could not sleep
because an alarm was set or not set,
because I had eaten too much
or not enough or I hadn't stretched

or I was almost cold or faintly overheated, over-
hearted with longing for my family back in Pittsburgh,
back in Detroit, back in Oshkosh, Wisconsin,
and Paw Paw, Michigan, and in the deep dark

ground, drifting forever away from me.
I no longer had pills. The tremble of panic
strummed taut strings till all was rigid,
brittle, the hairline crack

of sanity spreading with each blink,
each heart thud, each dry swallow
until I grabbed the baggie and spread red dirt
in an arc around my bed.

Cold turkeys gobbled at my sliding door,
steaming glass. I imagined spreading salt across
the icy sidewalk back in Pittsburgh
where my children slept, their soft breath holy

as all get-out. This is the part of the song
where the gospel choir sways into action,
kicks it into the high gear many of us die trying

to find, burning out the clutch of the heart,
the soul, the faint smell of burning rubber,
and we're stranded forever.

I woke up to the alarm
of a truck beeping reverse in morning's
definite light. When I rose, I wept

at the faint red half-circle in the faded green
carpet. The smirking genie. The shame
of the bargain. The broken hourglass.
The wall of abandoned crutches.

Lip Gloss, Belgium

The phone company sent me six bills, postage 44 cents
each, to tell me I owed 26 cents. Then they sent

a bill saying I owed $6.26. When I called to object,
I was phone-menued to a new dial tone.

I borrow my neighbor's dog for runs in the park
just to be able to hand back the leash and walk away.

My daughter pulls on my hair to make sure
I'm not a witch. She cried when I beat her

at ping-pong—the computer's red thing
just underlined that: I'm supposed to capitalize

Ping-Pong. Red Thing wants to be capitalized, too.
A train runs under my chair and crashes into my foot.

I wish I'd grown up in Ping Pong, Wisconsin.
Or Hyphen, Missouri. My daughter's been studying

the phrases of the moon (Red Thing didn't catch that one!)—
my favorite is Doth Hither! My hair's not falling out,

just stiffening white. I tried to keep the game close,
but that made it worse. I would've happily lost.

The soul is the size of a ping-pong ball with the consistency
of jello (Jell-O?). It's lit by a wick formed with the letters

of the first lie. The world says I owe it 26 cents.
To send it c/o Red Thing, AL. Maybe Red Thing

should just underline lies. I was born before
lip gloss was invented. I used to use an ink eraser

manufactured in Oxymoron, New Jersey—I believe
the soul of the nun who was my sixth-grade teacher

was made of that exact same material. My daughter's
asleep now. Someone is calling a dog, but the dog

isn't coming. Maybe the soul is a place where someone
is calling for us. No matter what we say, the voice

keeps calling—it could be dinner time or bath time.
We'll never know. Or maybe when we die, and our bodies

are taken to Lip Gloss, Belgium, we find out.
Or else, we meet some boring asshole who keeps insisting

we call it table tennis. When the moon's last dark smudge
becomes light, like a ping-pong ball rising off the table

toward the basement's spiky rafters,
nearly anything could happen.

Hit and Run

The girl was crossing the street, birthday cake in hand.
The bus against the curb blocked traffic.

> My daughter dances three nights a week
> with graceful insects—level three, purple leotards.

Last night playing softball in the park, I leaned
against the fence where the girl's friends left flowers.
You will never be forgotten, the scrawled sign read.

> I was dropping my daughter off at dance that night
> right after the accident. Body parts strewn across the road
> in front of the studio. Even the police looked stricken.
> I swerved around them, kept going. My daughter
> claims she closed her eyes and saw nothing.

At softball, I eyed the frayed flowers, the plaintive sign
streaked by rain. Liquid life goes on, and everyone
is forgotten. I was 2 for 3 and made a nice play
at second. I cannot tell you the final score.

> I cannot tell you who that birthday cake was for,
> splattered amid the gore. The ritual singing of sirens.

The other team had some asshole pitching,
whining about every call. Old guy my age
who should've known better than to care: Ball. Strike.
Safe. Out. Who cares? Nobody got hurt—
at our age, isn't that enough, oh worthy opponent?

> A severed leg in the road. You can still see
> the imperfect yellow circles drawn by police, fading.

Oh, dancing daughter. Watch me make a catch. Watch me
run the bases. Open your eyes, girl.

One Word

My brother lies in his hospital bed
steeped in the clammy smell
of the almost-dead. Stitches hang
stiff under his chin, a scraggly
Fu Manchu they sewed on him
fresh off life-flight, his motorcycle
mangled by a sixteen-year-old
running a stop sign. My brother
is simply/trying/to speak. To push out/
a single word. The breathing tube's
been removed—we thought when it came out
he'd be telling us he's going to be alright
or at least where it hurts, but his brain
still spun, weaving a fuzzy web.
We're bent over, smelling the pain, at his lips, so close
those stitches prick. He's making a noise
something like the Tin Man. But he's not saying oil me.
He's not saying—*What? Listen. C'mon, try again*—
it's more than a groan and less than satisfactory.
Like the slo-mo grunt of a tennis player so jazzed up
he can't just hit it and keep quiet. Like the door
to the principal's office swinging open
for you. *C'mon, open your eyes.*
Just one eye. A sound like grating bread crumbs.
An oral afterthought unfinished.
The squeaky chair you squirm in.
A dud firework. Six days, and they haven't given him
a bath—he reeks. His thing's beeping again
and where's the nurse and—wait—
We love you, can you hear us? It's less than a whistle
and more than maddening. The Tin Man's faux clumsy
rattling dance—that dude's going to Oz, so why not us,
we all have hearts. Brother, we'll make a deal
with the damn witch, trade her some of your neat handwriting

and good manners—broomstick, slippers—a package deal
for a little translation, a little more wet space
between dry lips for sound to slip out—anything,
anything, my eyes closed, concentrating on the subtle rise
and fall of what are less than syllables, but more
than random. Oh, my brother, we're lighting the torches
and heading out into the darkness to find the words
and bring them back to you.

On Tears

Tears do not add up with the firmness
of American quarters. Or pennies. Or dimes. They fall
with the urgency of escapees, no way to lose the dogs of grief
who will lick them up, swallow, and stand firm, panting, waiting
for more. Even Alice's pool of giant tears only measures
four inches deep. What if we all met in mourning and shed our tears
into a large hole and created a new Great Salt Lake? Well,
if the moon were a wafer of bread, and the salty pond
the broth of redemption, we might have something.
But there's no saving the moon. Somebody nibbling it
away each month. Or maybe the sky itself is the pool of tears,
and the stars grains of salt. Or okra in the soup.
Tears fall and evaporate so quickly nobody has time
to lick or collect them, label and study them under microscopes
for self-pity or self-righteousness. Even the drip from the faucet,
bigger than one tear. Is there anything sadder than a tear emerging
to weave down the landscape of the cheek, sometimes even
down the neck? Then another? If they don't fly off the chin.
If you don't have somebody with a tissue saying *there there*.
Once you reach a certain age, nobody says *there there*
ever again. Maybe that's sadder. The last *there*.
And you're on your own, spilling them into small droplets
on the floor or the rug or the cement or the car seat
or the gravestone. And you're swallowing hard
and they count for nothing.

Making a Case for the Letter

I open the October envelope from Linden, Michigan,
where my old friend Doug Johnson resides with his wife Marcy
who I haven't seen in twenty years though I did attend their wedding
in Detroit, December, 1977, when I had a suspicious moustache and a
    shiny disco
shirt purchased for the occasion, one-too-many buttons unbuttoned,
and picked up a nurse-friend of Marcy's and we ended up
in a car parked in her parents' driveway trying to have sex in
    December—
unsuccessful, despite good intentions and slippery clothing,
yet I promised to call her before going back to college but then
my friend Jack called from Alma to tell me my autumn girlfriend
Anne Devine had died in a car accident in Colorado, asleep in the
    back seat
as her aunt drove/crashed—*that fast*, he said, to say something—
and I rushed back to Alma early just to grieve with our common
    friends,
and though we weren't sleeping together at the time I may have been
her last lover—she was kind to my dog and all living creatures
and I cannot tell you why we broke up since our last conversation
was about borrowed records and Christmas plans because of course
we would see each other in January and, who knows, maybe try
    again—
when I open Doug's letter, a tiny yellow leaf falls onto my red kitchen
    table
because the leaf fell on the sheet of paper he was writing on
so he felt he should include it, and it made me think of that autumn
in 1977, and Anne, beautiful, with long blond hair, 6'1, like me,
so we saw eye to eye, touched hip to hip, and danced
at a bluegrass festival in Remus, Michigan, held on some guy's farm,
and made quiet love in the woods off the path in the middle of
    October
sunshine and held each other naked and warm on my old blue
    sleeping bag

and listened to the sweet whine of fiddles in the distance
and the world was spinning around our little circle of love
surrounded by tall trees, the wind gently dropping small yellow leaves
on top of us so that when she stood naked, her long blond hair
    speckled
with them, I thought for a moment to brush the leaves away
but then just lightly stroked her hair instead, leaves and all,
and maybe I called her a goddess.
Marcy said her friend understood why I didn't call back.
In the car, after giving up, she and I had smiled and laughed
at the odd contortions of our lust, and how we did not know each
    other.
Maybe we should just send each other envelopes of leaves,
eh, old friend? I shaved off the stupid moustache and never had
an occasion to wear that shirt again—who knows the last time
we're going to wear something? Oh, Anne,
long, long gone, the leaves still falling.

2. Foundation

Foundation

Thick gray cinder blocks
of a dead-dream basement
created a weedy pit
in the rubbled field behind
the mined parking lot
of boarded-up Bronco Lanes.
Even the bowlers
had abandoned us.

We stole the records
from the alley's jukebox
and frisbeed them into the wilds
of one of many unnamed fields
of Warren, Michigan.

Thin triangles and half moons, quarter
moons and mutant moons of black vinyl
emerged in the brown brittle
of fall before the snows fell.

In the pit, we puzzled out words
to songs that could cut.

▣

The sin pit nobody bothered
to rope off or fill in, empty skull
carved out by the economic hallucination
of somebody worse off than the rest of us—
us, who stayed, meeting
at the corner of Options Few
and Options None
to compare notes on where
it all went wrong.

It: the miracle of the American automobile.
The Car. Wheels. Ride. Check out my new ride!

We were confused. Who can blame us
for patching our souls in Bondo
while pissing on our own hearts.

◘

What we did down in the pit
depended on age and hour,
on the myth of parents
and the legend of Henry Ford,
on change for a twenty
and the quality of the drug,
the myth of reliability
and the legend of the one
who got away.

It stunk/stank/stinks:
vomit, bad poetry, mold, cold,
steaming internal organs,
broken fizz in the fissures
of bad wine, beer, the charred
remains of despair's good times.

Like the dark corner of the church
where you once confessed,
where you once believed.
Spoiled meat and spoiled
surprises. Dancing hot dogs
and sperm in a bun.

When the wind blew right
it still did not matter. You stood
or crouched or huddled or circled
below wind.

◘

In winter, we made snow
devils, then kicked their asses.
In summer, we lit trash fires
and scorched the bricks.

The police never left their cars
unless blood was visible.
Or somebody knew somebody
or Officer Hyperbole was on patrol.

If you fought someone
in the pit, mercy bled
into an ugly pool
and declared no winner.

What happened in the pit
did not stay in the pit.
It crawled out and slithered
through weeds, through drafty
cracks of our windows,
through the peepholes
of our splintered wooden doors.

◘

I could draw you a map
write you a guidebook
and you still would not
find us. We became weeds.
We snorted and smoked
and injected weed killer,
imagining it made us stronger.

We spray-painted the obvious,
the oblivious, onto bricks,

and it dripped down until it stopped,
like unfinished cave drawings
of the extinct or merely bored.

I never got high enough
to see the dream house rising above us—
windows without bars,
bathrooms with the enormous tubs
of the rich and famous.

We were illiterates or mutes
in the language of luxury.
We could not even conjure
desire into four walls and a roof.

We were demolition experts
admiring the job
we never had to do.

◘

What happened in the pit
when my friend Carl's older brother Curt
lured my friend Larry's little sister Kate
down with the candy of cigarettes
and the charm of a ring-nosed bull

and she emerged half-naked, half-
gone, fully ruined, no one
was arrested or even questioned

till somebody shot Curt.

◘

One long wail. Muddy boots
of retreat. Footprints frozen

into angles of the Hurry Up,
the Fuck Me.

If someone gives you lemons
you squeeze the juice into the eyes
of whoever fucked you up like that
then you spike the lemonade.

We could not scrape or claw
our way up the rough bricks
of what we had inherited.

All of our answers were incomplete.
No multiple choices.
None of the above and all of the above
meant the same thing.

◙

Why did we have such a crush
on cruelty? It held us up.
It had our back. It never let us down.

I'm gonna *fuck* you *up*
the rhythm we danced to
taking turns leading

the parade to the sin pit
where sin in fact did not exist

or, if it did, was stoned
out of its mind.

◙

We were the buried treasures
of our parents' nightmares

who grew up to tattoo the dead-end
maps onto our chests.

X marks the spot.
X where someone had once dug,
foolish enough to think
it'd be that simple.

Six feet under, ten feet
under. Who's measuring,
who's counting, eh, Curt?
Eh, Kate?

◘

We christened the bricks nightly,
renamed the pit with endless
variations of jokes that prompted
only cold barking. The sprinkling
of glass, the only rain recognized
in the unwritten book
of the electric shock, the bible
of the pit and its many gospels,
its bullshit epistles, its heavenly
toxic fumes.

Your foundation must be solid
or it's all coming down on you.
Start with the roof and see what happens.
Leave it open to the sky
and see what happens.

I shook up cans of spray paint
and danced to the rattle inside.
The Lord needed a new target
and we were his servants.

◘

Upon this brick I have built
my curse.

Weeds can grow absolutely
anywhere. Nothing can kill
them—we counted on that.
On our fingers and our toes.
We counted on the rapture
to lift us up to ground level.

We walked on water. The great flood
receded and left the foundation
of this ark. Wherever the actual ark drifted to,
it is written that Noah unloaded there
to bring back the good stuff, pure, uncut,
to those who could pay. If only
he could find us down here

we'd kill the motherfucker
for taking the last two of everything.

3. One Arm Raised

The Geography of Detroit

requires no assembly. Requires the stubborn faith
of the abandoned child at the locked church door
clutching his get out of jail free card. Requires
the illusion of covering your tracks
when no one gives a damn to start with.

I felt I was off to a good start, then ended up
with swearing and a preposition. That's how
it works here, 6 Mile Road to 36 Mile Road,
praying for the optical illusion of cliffs
to justify free fall.

Someone carved the history of the auto industry
on a piece of rock salt. That piece of salt
went on to melt a small slice of ice
and contribute to the construction
of the world's largest pothole.

I was going to say, "That's another story,"
but there is no other story.
Going to need some gas soon.
Shouldn't be the last word
but it is.

Company Men

My grandfather worked at Packard's for 43 years.
My father worked at Ford's for 35.
One brother worked at Big Boy's for 20
then Chrysler's for 15 and counting. Another
has worked at GE for 35 and counting.
The third has worked at Chevron for 30 and counting.
I have worked at Carnegie Mellon for 32
and counting and counting.

We do not look for new jobs.
We take what they give us. We drink our coffee
black. We tip the mailman at Christmas. We mow
our lawns and prop up our homes, reluctant
to call an electrician or plumber. We believe in
fixing what's broke. Not in cafeteria lines or IOUs.
We pack our own lunches. We are proud of taking it
without complaint.

We believe in God's dance floor
and the boogie-woogie of interest-
bearing checking accounts.
We accept wooden nickels
and trim them into five toothpicks.
We like toothpicks. If a restaurant offers none,
we are permanently suspicious. We fly our flags
on holidays but not bumper stickers. We do not
believe in bumper stickers of any kind.
We believe in turtle wax and in all things turtle
because we are plodding in our hard shells
toward the finish line.

When Packard went belly-up, my grandfather lost
his pension. He lived off Social Security
for thirty more years. He handed out dollar bills

to his grandsons like tickets to the big game
he was unable to go to himself
due to prior commitments. And we took
those dollar bills and saved them
for rainy days, for it was always a sunny day
when we got dollars from our grandfather.

Nobody has a gold watch. But we will tell you
the time. And if we are stupidly smug
about our years of seniority, forgetting
the lesson of our grandfather, forgive us.
We are not squeaky wheels. We are silent
even on each other's porches, analyzing mortar
between bricks for signs of crumbling.

Our companies moved us up,
then stopped moving us up. And so
we listen to the young bucks
and nod as they tell us how to do our jobs.
We do not discuss our jobs.
We leave our jobs where they belong.

Two of us laid off now, the counting suspended
due to inclement weather or unreliable mathematicians,
a wrong turn or global hijinks, we can't be sure,
scraping our fingers against the mortar.

The story says the tortoise beat the hare,
but that's not what our bankbooks say.
We are never late, God willing—
though we're not sure he is.

One Arm Raised

In the park yesterday, I taught my daughter
to make dandelion chains. Our jeans smudged
yellow with the jazz of spring. Only a few puffed out
for wishes, and we didn't need many.

We set our necklaces on a playground bench
and tried to find and lose each other
among castles and dinosaurs. She spun me dizzy
on the merry-go-round, and I staggered X's
till my eyes turned back to O's. Good
for a laugh. Our imagined kites flew in the lazy sun.
We slurped at the fountain flowing for summer.

A young man staggered toward us, one arm raised,
blood dripping. He knelt in the dirt and ran the cut
under water. He asked for tissue. I had none.
He took off a sock and wrapped it around
his sliced hand. Between thumb and index finger.
Where you'd get cut reaching against a knife.

He was a lump of dark misery I could not
explain. Misery or menace—who can judge
with a five-year-old daughter upside down
on the bars, swinging, staring?

We edged away from the bloody sock.
On the bench, our yellow chains lay broken,
scattered by some curious child or creature.

We gathered new batches to weave together
at home, but today they sit loosely piled
on our porch, color draining.

Feed Corn

My brother, my friend Bill, and I left the factory simultaneously
in an act of speed-laced bravado and drove east from Detroit
in search of an ocean and a comfortable state of oblivion

but before we arrived, my brother fell off the car roof
on a remote backroad in New York State when I drove
under the low-hanging branches of the rest of our lives.

After we stole corn from a field and boiled it into oblivion
over our campfire, it was still hard and inedible as crow,
though crows and pigs would not have minded devouring it.

Kumbaya indeed. At the campground we stole
the underwear of two Canadian girls. Did we?
Maybe we just grabbed them off their tent ropes where they

hung drying, examined them, then tossed them
like penalty flags. Maybe we just looked and giggled like boys.
We were not un-drunk, and my memory is biased on the side

of 3D glasses and idealized soundtracks. Here,
we take a big jump into my uncle's boat in Massachusetts
where he drank us under the table, and since under the table

was water, we swam to shore while he threatened to get us
jobs we'd hate as much as he hated his.
Maybe you got your feet wet on that jump.

While you're wet, let's jump again
to watch the sunrise with a sad school teacher
camping on her own who had room in her tent for me.

Camping by myself in a state park was added to my list
of depressing things I vowed I'd never do. Oh, I've done
them all, that's the short version. The long version

is still being edited as we speak. As I speak. I'm taking
the dust off the needle then poking myself in the eye
with that needle then falling into a haystack of needles

from which I will emerge with tattoos and humility.
But that's years from *this* now. We drive home
and back to work because the truth is

that the layoff was temporary, and we were called back.
I could make a list of many people I would like
to call me back—just as I'm going out the door,

just as I'm getting in the car, just as I'm getting
on the bus, train, plane. I walked on a lot of eggs
and broke every one of them, so I was lucky

to get a wave, or one of those half-smile grimaces
that suggested if I lingered one more minute
someone would scream at high decibels.

Hearing Protection Required. Today, I'm wondering
how much hearing I lost. Is there a finite amount
of shame in each lifetime? We did not

exchange phone numbers or addresses, and I forgot
her name within forty-eight hours. She may have
forgotten mine sooner as she pulled up her stakes.

It's the only sunrise I've seen above the ocean.
I think sunsets are supposed to be the bigger deal
though that's a lot further from Detroit

as the crow flies or the dog dies or my uncle lies
about his Navy days. Keep moving—I know
that doesn't make much sense. Before I go

I want to tell you about Elvis dying. It's been in my head
all along. I almost didn't want to mention it, given
his cartoon stature: the fried pb-and-banana sandwiches,

the monkeys, dying on the toilet. My sister loved Elvis.
No wonder she ended up a Republican. Okay, okay—
cheap shot. I think all shots should be more expensive.

We heard the news on one of the three stations left
on the radio in my Plymouth Satellite—the antenna removed
in an unfortunate parking-lot altercation.

We called it our Options Limited World Tour.
Very small world, I know, but shrinkage, etc. We knew
our sister was bawling her eyes out back in Detroit

and that her tears were genuine human tears, so we didn't even
joke about it, though back home, we teased her without
mercy. I never knew what she saw in Elvis. But I imagined her

inconsolable on her flowery bedspread in the tiny room
she shared with my grandmother. I felt like an alien stone
had landed in my chest, that weighted loss I had yet to feel

since I'd believed in no one or nothing my entire life
like that. Not even God. It's no wonder that we accidentally
ended up in Canada as we listened to the news.

Love Me Tender, Hound Dog, Amen.

Record Accumulation

My family's stranded in a state park lodge,
a thick, tumbling blizzard swirling
us snow-blind and silent in its cocoon.
We resort to television. At home

we just watch movies. Soon, my daughter's
imagining ads for every item in our room.
The cynical patter of an eight-year-old

soaks into the clumsy, smudged curtains. My son
pockets the *Do not disturb* sign as a souvenir.
Snow too deep for sleds flaunts its sunny brilliance

like a spoiled genius on a quiz show. We pretend
the game room below the lobby does not exist.
The gift shop does not carry antacids.
The kids each buy a bag of rocks.

Our car is a small white hill
in the parking lot. Three deer stare at us
through the sliding glass door.
Maybe soon we'll start talking about God.

Exterior with Quiet

St. Rose of Lima Parish, Detroit, 1919–1989

The house of my birth has floated away
into the Detroit River, like most of the East Side.
I wish I could imagine it landed safely in Canada
to start a new life, but years ago my aunt watched it
burn to the ground.

My grandfather traded vegetables for dental work
for his children until the rottenness scale tipped over
like the cart he wheeled to the street each morning.
His house stood defiantly abandoned for years.

After we'd shipped him out overnight delivery to a safe zone,
he returned for something he imagined he'd forgotten
and met a minister, a prostitute, and a drug dealer,
and they collaborated on a bad joke that lacked
a punch line, the thing he forgot.

▣

The math of the heart, the random numbers,
the prime ghosts of erasures, the imaginary
healing of the bruises.

They pulled down the old church like a diseased elephant.
Like a gray tooth, like a busted equation,
like the thrown fight between religion and economics.

The street's many ruins rose up
to swarm over holy rubble,
to say *you are just like us*, to say *God
has left the building or else got crushed.*

◘

I blame the messenger
because I cannot find who sent him.
Perhaps no one.

Truth has a smell
like a book ruined by rain.

A lone bird's cry, amplified
by the lack of shelter,
carries over the concrete carnage:

I used to
there used to
we used to

◘

Out here, silence scrapes its knuckles
in an attempt at prayer.

Silence has a way of forgetting.
The hands of silence either surrender

or nestle tightly around your throat.
So quiet, tall weeds and broken bricks
have become lovers, the wind

both imaginary and inescapable—
no one feels it, and nothing rises to stop it.

◘

The nonrandom numbers on those houses
are buried, and the mail delivered to outer space
or made into origami boats and launched

into the Detroit River. The river that has flowed,
continues to flow. Its job is to have nothing to say.
It says it well and without complaint.

The old maps are the prayer books
of the faithful and the heathens both.

◘

Somebody beat up my grandmother for her cheap pearls,
and she forgot the magic words of her name.
Her old change purse opened, a sad, empty clam.

Hungover the day we moved them,
I burned my tongue on hot coffee.

◘

Oh, it's not so bad. History has a way
of removing the blood
fixing the teeth
piling up the debris
into neat little castles.

Oh, it's not so bad.
I've got my litany of vacant lots
squared off with silence
and blurred with angry tears.

My ears hurt with listening—
when a car goes by
they rupture with grief,
they explode with the ordinary
rattle and hiss.

◘

Ah, dusted grief.
Truth like incense lingering
in the empty prayer.

The numbers tumble
into their own ironic graffiti.
I'm listening for the sound of footsteps
not the bird of my own heart.

Taking the Leap

My faith has gone to the dogs.
Dogs will eat their own vomit
if you let them. *That's* faith.
They swallowed my faith,
and I'm not sure they kept it down.

Fifteen, drunk, I crashed through
the hallway plaster to avoid my mother's
kiss. She'd jumped off a chair in front of me.

She's eighty now, and blind.
My son, fifteen, forgot to take out
the garbage last night. I'd offered
to help him earlier, but he declined.
Declining is the slant here.

I'd tap-dance through hell
to get a smile out of him.
Is he drinking yet?
I can still jump off chairs.

I'd jump off a chair to surprise my mother
if she could see me, if I could be sure
she would not fall.

We never gave my son faith in God
so he has not lost it. Just his faith in us.
Fragile and *faith* get rewound, redefined,
refined. My dog Prince once chewed
Jesus off the cross. Oh, we had a laugh
over that. Helluva way to get resurrected.

I edited out the part about being drunk
for the family oral history. Just a cute little tale
of a man-boy not wanting to kiss his mother.

Last time my son and I embraced was after
he ran away, then came home. That night
as the porch light glowed above me,
I sat waiting with folded fists
for him to leap back into our lives.
I may have prayed.

She pulled me out of the wall.
My ass covered in plaster dust.
Everyone admired the empty tomb
except my father who stuck his fingers in
to assess the damage.

My mother got another shot
in her hip last week so she can keep
that wheelchair in the garage.

It was hard throwing Jesus away,
even a chewed-up Jesus. No way
was he going back up on that cross.

Last week, a girl sprayed my son with perfume
as a joke. He wouldn't come near me. Sat alone
in the back seat as I drove him home.

We're in free fall here. We're tearing the walls
back to the studs. We're excavating for relics.
We have no evidence. We've stopped taking pictures.

What did my mother see then? Why wouldn't
I let her kiss me goodbye?

I've got enough sight left. The dogs
bark cold outside. Their breath rises
toward the streetlight and disappears.

He tells me he's heard all my stories,
though I know that's not true. He broke a chair
last week just by sitting down.

My father sealed up the hole, though you could still see
the faint outline of where I fell.

He barges into my room without knocking,
but won't open his door to talk, tries to slam it on me.
We fight about what we can measure—sleep, food, time.

My father hit me for the last time
when I was fifteen. I'm sure I deserved it.
An open hand to the cheek.

My son jolted away from my hand
on his shoulder on Christmas day
but opened all the gifts.

We've got baby Jesus here in the house
of unbelievers. Sometimes a good story
can keep you going a long time:

I tap-danced through hell
and even Satan applauded. I lifted
my guardian angel's robe

and saw nothing. Jesus escaped
out of a hole in the wall. My mother
got her sight back. She threw away her walker,

and sang, dancing with me like back
when I was little—laughing, thrilled
to be in her arms.

We lost our wings a long time ago, my son,
so take me in your arms, catch me
as I fall.

Church Reform

ghost: 7. (obsolete) The Holy Ghost

Sister Ingrid informed us
that the Pope decided the Holy Ghost
was now the Holy *Spirit*
and anyone who forgot
would get five yardsticks
across the knuckles.

◧

But I believe in the Holy Ghost,
having seen gentle doves
and flaming tongues of a kind.

The Papal Office of Connotation
got lost in translation. I have been
lost in translation my entire life—
peanut butter on my sleeve,
milk moustache.

◧

You look like you've seen a ghost.

Which looks exactly how?
Haunted=Alive≠Faith.

Beyond the pale.

◧

Oh Lord, my wings, overrun
with maggots, dropped

to the dirt. And then
I was truly free.

◘

We shouted *spirit*
in our prayers, shrill
cheerleaders for Christ.

Sister Ingrid became petrified
then transferred to heaven
on the Barge of Holy Sisters
steered by Jerry J the Janitor.

It says so in the Good Book
transcribed by the Langley brothers
who all went bald by age twelve
and moved to Indianapolis.

◘

Life is a rosary. The world is a killer pill.
The Holy Ghost is *built for comfort
not for speed.* The Holy Ghost
believes that sugar is good for you.
The Holy Spirit is a vegan jogger.

◘

Five with the yardstick,
and I'm sitting in the amen corner
facing the cork bulletin board,
thumb tacks holding up lists of sins.
Is the Holy Ghost the bird of memory?

◘

The Papal Committee on Holy Water
vs. the Cardinal Committee on the Texture
of the Communion Wafer. Tag Team,
Texas Death Match. Refereed by Joseph
and his coat of many contradictions.

◘

The Holy Ghost never interrupts.
It makes me laugh, alone in bed.
It is the Joke on Everybody.

◘

Woooooooooooo! Boooooo!
Scare me, Holy Ghost, c'mon,
I'm ready for you! Bring it on,
Holy Ghost! I love
your connotative aspects!

The voices of all my dead friends
in the limbo choir chant
How low can you go?

◘

I've tucked my shirt in
and wet down my hair.
I've tied my tie tight enough
to choke back tears. I have polished
my black shoes with my tongue.
Yes, Sister. No, Sister.

◘

Rate your doubt on a scale of one to ten.
The Holy Ghost smells like lavender and shit.

The Holy Ghost sighs in the first breath
of every child and in the last breath of the dying.

◘

When I crack my knuckles,
it releases a little more venom.
It's a long process. Don't wait up
for me. You'll be asleep when I get home.
I'm going out with the Holy Ghost
in a car loaded with broken clocks
to drive through the sands of the broken
hourglass—we're going to go confuse the Pope
while he's counting souls. Make him start
all over again.

Those of Us Without AC

My childhood dog Prince scratches at the door of my dreams.
Goodnight, Sweet Prince, you champeenship leg-humper—
that rhythm, the only metrics I've ever needed. I get lost
counting the stresses of the bass in the juiced-up motorized
thump machine idling in front of the building across the street
either dropping off or picking up drugs at 3 a.m.
Prince is humping to the beat in some doggie porn film.
Does a dog get turned on watching other dogs?
I'm sure they've done studies. It's 95° in June in Pittsburgh,
and that ain't right. Fan of God take away the sins of the world.
Why won't anybody let me say Amen?
We're baking Shrouds of Turin into our sheets tonight
while the young and brave and passionate
may be melting themselves into small puddles
where exotic creatures with life spans lasting till dawn
breed themselves into oblivion.
The night's dark windows and the air studded with humid ghosts
leave us gasping for life. I want to dream the simple dreams
of a dog, my legs dancing and twitching. That'd be enough,
you old dog, Prince. Prince of Darkness, Prince of Everlasting
First-Death tears. If you wrapped me in this wet sheet
and threw me out the window, I would fly.
It's a matter of faith, like anything
with God and dog in it.

Treaty

March 2003

Given the recent abuses of math
and the blue spinning record of grief,
given the severe sexless arching
of the eyebrows and the counting of syllables,
the blackballing of rant, I invoke the dark shuffle
of a homeless man named Henry
and the syllabic tint and glint of bullets, the soft
thud of the muted unrecorded blow.

Given the lack of eyes on the ball
and the hysterical shredding of money
and tongues, I surrender the magnetic strip
of the credit card and the grim
shapeless weight of erosion.

Given the party of the first part
is keeping the rest of us awake
with its jolly smug lip service,
I pledge the service of my lips
to love and sinful pleasure.

Given the endless blessings
of America demanded of God
at every public occasion,
I pledge to blaspheme with forethought
and malice in the interests
of fairness and balance.

Given the Powerball and the nuclear
shenanigans, give me Stubby Kaye singing
"Sit Down You're Rockin' the Boat."

Given the poison in the well
and the fox in the henhouse,
I pledge to crow at the break of dawn.

Given the hair rising on my neck
every time the President speaks,
I pledge to earn every demerit
available on my report card.

Given the lack of hullabaloo and shindig
and the hiss of static on my radio,
I pledge the funky chicken, the tighten up,
the bump and the twist.
Dancing in my living room,
I promise to turn up the music
and invite you in.

4. Love Poem with Pesticide

Love Poem with Pesticide

Morning frost on our side of the hill
until sun angles down through the white flutter
of the first blooming almond trees,
now shining through *here*.

I've been cupping your breasts
and singing off-key. Now we stand
half-dressed in the open field—
joyful shiver and squint.

Above us on the hill, our neighbor
wrestles his sprayer off the truck.
Everything we have not risked
we've abandoned to be here together.

He nods, we wave. The poison
mist descends through the trees
in an unapologetic, almost
beautiful rainbow down toward us.

We linger.

Riding the Bench

I was adept at guzzling quart bottles
of Colt 45. G.I.Q.'s—before the era of the 40 oz.
I thought it was military, but it meant Great Imperial Quart.
Perhaps you knew that, or perhaps you never rode
the bench. *Rode* implies skill, as in *rode a horse*.
I sat far from the coach, close to the door.

Somebody claimed a hole in the janitor's closet
exposed the girl's locker room. I never found it.
But with time on my hands, or in close proximity
to my hands, it was something to imagine.
Like who designed that jolting buzzer for substitutions
or timeouts or one-and-one situations.
I wanted a one-*on*-one situation. On the bench
I had a clear shot at the cheerleaders
cross court. I wanted them on my side, sticking
their cute little butts in my face. I deserved
to ride the bench with an attitude like that.

They gave me number 51. Never accept 51.
Quit first. Or try to trade down.
The referee's hand signaled a foul on me:
5 fingers, then 1. I fouled as often as possible
during my 67 seconds, my 51 seconds.
My mop-up role. I got mop sores, saddle sores,
and just plain sore, so I began guzzling Colt before games
and burping in the face of Dick Randall
the 11th man. I was 12th. Dick was disgusted,
but why tell the coach? Then *he'd* be the last guy.

I'd like to say I played better drunk, but I rarely played
at all. Dock Ellis claimed he pitched a no-hitter on acid.
I trotted that out in my defense as I trotted onto the court.
I got 85 cents an hour at Dairy Queen for mopping up,

but it was closed for winter. I stayed on the team
to avoid taking gym class where I got my ass kicked
by larger boys who did not play basketball.

The gym ceiling lights were covered by cages
but no one ever threw the ball that high.
I often tried before practice. Like that imaginary
hole in the janitor's closet. I was a good
mopper-upper, wringing that mop to beat the band,
the pep band. They were all stoned anyway,
tooting and honking at cheerleaders.
I was always fresh for after-game parties.
Malt liquor's stronger than beer. You might
know that. If you've ever ridden a colt before.
I never threw a no-hitter. I never got to pitch.

I was number 51 in every sport. I warmed the bench,
not really riding it, though if riding were involved,
I would've said *Whoa, boy!* or *Heel, boy!*
I was 15, my number in reverse. I was aging
that fast, not even working up a sweat.
What was I doing down on that bench?
From this distance, all I can tell is that the boy
needed a haircut and decent sneakers.
He needed to shout, *Throw me the damn ball!*
I should've at least been the 11th man.

The cheerleaders bought my ice cream cones.
I was master of the DQ Swirl. The coach, the boss,
the driver's ed instructor, conspired against me.
It was all in my head. And nothing was in my head.
I slept through algebra—15/51. 45—and spent earth science
looking at Connie Mullin's ass in the seat
in front of me. She wore hip-huggers. I wore 51.
I was neither great nor imperial. I never saddled up
the palomino. I was riding the jackass express
into the quicksand of bad grades and miscellaneous

misdemeanors. *Put me in, Coach*, I should've said.
I scored one point the whole season.
That point is this:

My Two Aunts

work at Burger King and McDonalds.
One in Newark, the other in Memphis.
My two aunts married two drunks—
one died, the other disappeared.

My two aunts are two alcoholics,
recovering. One dates a blind man.
The other dates memory:
her husband's final day
breathing his own blood.

Their alcoholic sons
have married and divorced.
Their children are sad and overweight
they are tall and stutter
they have imaginary illnesses
they blame their fathers
they blame their mothers
they smoke one endless cigarette.

But my two aunts,
they are saying *May I help you?*
and *Big Mac and fries?*
and *Whopper and fries?*
They are amazed by and resigned to
the goofy hats and polyester slacks.

They take orders from bosses
younger than their children.
They pledge allegiance to the burger corps.
After work they put their feet up
and reach for the imaginary drink.

One lost the condo paying off
shared credit cards after the divorce.
The other lost the house after the husband
lost his salesman's job after 27 years,
lost his factory job after six months,
ended up a janitor swigging wine
in a broom closet.

My two aunts take off their sour uniforms
and sleep or don't sleep, depending.
Big Mac and a Quarter Pounder.
Whopper. Itchy collar, swollen feet.

No more Cheerios for dinner
no more shakes and instant regrets
no more half-gallon-vodka guilt and lies.
One aunt bites holes in her lips
and takes community college classes in math.
The other started aerobics
with matching leotard and sweatband.

It's a matter of time,
they both say, *I'm getting on*
my feet again. AA, the church.
Belief, addiction,
addiction, belief.
May I help you please?
Please, may I help you?

One aunt wants her marriage
annulled: they were teenagers and not
in their right mind for thirty years.
The other says she's stopped visiting
the grave but hasn't.

My two aunts are getting
their lives together.

They have shed their soggy dreams
they are selling hamburgers
in America for minimum wage
they are trying to shed
their scales and bad news.

If only they could give up
on bad news, swear it off.
What put them here
pressing buttons, handing out change?
Thank you, yes, thank you.
Here is your order.

My two aunts smoke now,
more than they ever drank.
My two aunts, one way or another
we will kill them.

The Family Price

My nephew bought my father's pickup, then promptly
sold it for blue-book value and bought

what? Where is he, the boy, 25, pretending to play drums,
weaving lies together like a summer-camp lanyard,

cruising right over the tangled mistakes? He's recording
a CD as we speak, a virtual CD spinning in his head

under the pressure of the tongue stud, the lip ring,
the other hidden punctures. What's it called, global

something—where your car tells you where you're at?
We don't have it. My father's doing his best to shrug.

He reluctantly just disposed of a fifty-year-old refrigerator.
No room for a backup in their tiny trailer. No need

for a pickup. My nephew says he's going to send me
a CD when it's done. He's calling on a cellphone

six states and thirty-seven time zones away
or right next door. He wants to know how I got straight

way back when. I wander through the house, searching
for a clear connection, but already he's breaking up,

sparking off into another absent night. It's not enough to say
I just did it, but I do. I did. My own kids want to know

who's on the phone. Or was—he's gone. My father got
a sedan. Easier on my mother's hip. My brother

should be the one taking the call, nodding into space.
But he's off clocking hours on some factory floor,

and I'm the family designated driver on the twisted road
to recovery. Not recovery—a flood, and you're not insured.

Nothing to do but put it all out for the trash and start over.
It's with you and not with you.

See why I had to hang up? Yeah, *I* hung up
on *him*. The pickup's gone. Family price.

My father cared for that truck like the old refrigerator.
A man of vehicles and appliances—kids don't work

the same way. I never blamed him. You start digging
that hole, and pretty soon all you're doing is tossing dirt

up in the air—it lands on your head, buries you.
My kids are nine and eleven. *Drugs are bad, kids. Yeah.*

That was your cousin Fred. I knew better than to ask him
to visit. He started singing me one of those tunes.

I liked it a little too much. Even now,
I'm humming it.

Good Reception

The TV repairman took our set away
and never brought it back. My mother
knew he was a drunk. Wanted to help
and look where it got us—TV limbo.
He also sold guns. Sunshine's Guns
and TV Repair. You'd think
he'd have made a million.

I worked in a liquor store. He'd stop in daily
and laugh when I asked about our TV.
He had a shop full of them,
outdated with layered silence and dust.

I'd overcharge him when he bought
anything to go with his bottle (he knew *that* price).
One Christmas, my father finally bought
our first colored set: everybody red with anger
or embarrassment, green with envy or nausea.
We never took anything back.

We took whatever they were dishing out.
Took it like a man, took it like a woman.
Took it, and took it again. *It's not like
he cheated us*, my mother said. *I never paid him
nothing. He just got himself*

a broke TV. Mr. Sunshine got himself
shot one day, but he didn't even die.
Not like TV's thirty or sixty minutes,
then closure. Out of the hospital in three weeks,
stocking up at the liquor store.
His place never reopened. Insurance
money. He disappeared. Some said he paid

somebody to shoot him. Could he have gotten
that drunk? The store's changed hands and locks
many times since, but the bars on the windows remain.
You need them to sell TVs and guns and liquor.
Your name could be Sunshine or Shit. My mother
believed every salesman was a fortune teller
and they were always right. My father thought

they saw him coming, and they did. The contrast knob
never worked on that old b&w. It was like peering through
thick fog. We could get channel 9 from Canada
if we folded the foil on our rabbit ears
into the shape of Jesus Christ.
They were calmer in Canada. We liked their anthem.
They had puppets that spoke French
and girls in black leotards doing the limbo
for Captain Jolly and Poopdeck Paul.

Okay, Mr. Sunshine hit on my mother.
I'm not sure what happened, but that's why
she never went back for the set. I found out
when he got shot. The police had questions.
We were instructed to amuse ourselves in the basement.
The neighbors had a field day with that episode,
a block-party hootenanny do-si-do.

Name three things wrong with this picture
and win another picture. My father drank Windsor
Canadian, which was not as good as Canadian Club,
much less Crown Royal, but still an extravagance
in our family. Amber over ice, sloshing against
the sides of the glass as the waves crashed
into our boat. We weren't in any Club.
I knew the subtle Canadian distinctions. I became
an expert on longing—no deposit, no return.

We listened to the muffled voices above us.
I could say we mimicked the puppets
who spoke French or prayed to Jesus
or that I saw my first female breasts
on channel 9 and that Captain Jolly got busted—
no more Popeye cartoons for him.
And at least some of that would be true.

I sold liquor for years. Steady work
with secret benefits and obvious liabilities.
Plenty of sunshine, plenty of nothing.
My parents never told us anything.
There was no gun in our house.
We never made the evening news.

45 RPM: Side A/Side B

A. PLAY LOUD "INSTANT KARMA"
JOHN ONO LENNON

Who on earth do you think you are? A superstar? So alright you are.
    John Lennon

I had no idea what "Instant Karma" was.
I knew a girl, Carlina, who survived
the accident that killed Kenny Sadowski,
ninth-grade president. He rolled over a Chevy
borrowed from his older brother.

The Catholic church next to the public high school
threw a youth dance with no assistant principals
to check the breath and stagger
of the Underage Drinkers of America.
The panicked nuns covered their veiled ears.
The mother superior performed a wild arm-dance
for the sloppy rockers on the old church's makeshift stage
but they would not lower the volume.

Kenny grew a moustache at age 15. That got him
elected and able to buy liquor. A vote for Kenny,
a vote for turning it up. We elected him
to a short wasted life. I wasn't in that car
due to lack of room. Carlina got religion
and lost her slithering dance moves and 96%
of the vote. No required age for wising up.
The Invincibles, featuring future members
of the Factory Rats.

The nuns who had terrorized us through eighth grade
had lost permission to send us to The Office.
To call on a Higher Power.
Have you got the spirit? Yeah, man.

Let the freshmen show it.
A little louder now. A little softer now.
His old teacher got his name wrong
at the reunion—*that boy who died.*

B. PLAY SOFT "WHO HAS SEEN THE WIND?"
YOKO ONO LENNON

Who has seen the wind? Neither you nor I.
    Yoko Ono

My girlfriend Jane Shizuka
had long black hair like Yoko
and we sure had fun in bed the one time
we had a bed, my parents out of town,
my deaf grandmother asleep upstairs.
I had no band to break up. Her boyfriend, Barry,
who later came out, had given Jane the crabs
and self-doubt, and she gave them to me.

After Lennon's murder, they turned
him into a saint when he was an asshole
just like us. He dissed God, and that was cool
with me and Jane. We didn't have no beef
with Yoko except she couldn't sing. Better
to leave them wanting more. Jane left me
wanting more. Not more crabs. More Jane.
The crabs were easy enough to get rid of,
but not the ones I imagined for months.

We didn't talk about peace. The war was time
zones away. My older brother with the bad
tattoo was the only one who went. Now
who was going to buy for us? We were cliff-
dwellers with our backs to the cave entrance.
We talked a lot about sex. That Jane,

she was a talker. Thirty years later, she takes
my breath away. Or maybe I'm just holding it.

The Shizukas, the only Japanese family around,
but I didn't consider that—I was considering
sex with Jane. It was a narrow range: PLAY IT LOUD.
We rode around a lot in Jane's car-ma.
We were not super-star-mas. Jane and I liked cigarettes
and complete silence. We liked to PLAY IT SOFT too,
soft spots rare on our pitted concrete streets.
Her father spoke English as an interplanetary language.
I have no idea what he did or how they ended up
in Warren, Michigan, where many hated
the Japanese because they made better cars.
I never asked. Because we were—right—
we were having sex. John and Yoko's Bed-In
was a big hit with us. The front seat of her VW Bug
was unkarma-fortable. Jane was small, like Yoko.
Is still small, wherever. Lansing, last I heard.

We once took a balloon to a restaurant.
We could be cute! Nobody cared!
Japanese! We ate pancakes with a balloon!
They served us cold coffee! We left a balloon tip!
I hope, wherever she is, she still lets her hair grow
down to her ass. Because, and this is my point,
when we walked down the street together,
her arm around my waist, and I tried to take
small steps to match hers, or she tried to take
long strides to match mine—cold out, and maybe
her nose or my nose was running, and we imagined
running away to Toledo or Cleveland or even Pittsburgh,
and Barry's name was briefly erased
from the blackboard of our young lives,
and as I turned to watch her walk up
the steps to her house, her hair
trailing behind her, I could,
I *could* see the wind.

Recreational Trail

The Eliza Furnace Trail is commonly known as the Jail Trail because it ends near the Allegheny County Jail in downtown Pittsburgh.

An Amish family of eight on the Jail Trail,
led astray from the bus station by directions
from a street-side Messiah selling ragged flowers
sewn from frayed escape ropes,
is striding straight at me. *Whoa!*
I shout to my inner Amishness.

The Monongahela River. Monongahela
means *peed on* in the language
of those living in cardboard near
the station, bogged down in the lack
of subtlety, degrees of despair.

I pass the Amish family of nine. Or seven.
At least six. In their hats and bonnets and long dresses,
sweating like pigs, like the rest of us, in August's un-
godly heat. Long dark lives. What do they make
of the cardboard huts? The amateurs and semi-pros
huddled around the station? The Amish only come
to Pittsburgh to go to Children's Hospital.
An Amish kid in Children's—the resort
of last resort.

I'm wearing a t-shirt that says
I'm with Shithead though I'm alone—
buying drugs, okay? They got 'em down here
on half-a-dozen corners within a quarter mile.
I get them downtown instead of in the neighborhood.
Makes it seem temporary.

I ask the Amish if they need directions.
They consult, and decide not.

A hooker dressed Amish could make
good money down here. I'd like to borrow
one of their cool hats, and a couple of official
prayers. By now, you might guess
I'm unreliable. On the Jail Trail.
Drug money in my pocket
folded, ready to go.

The Worn Knees and Elbows of My Alcoholic Uncles

On family occasions, they bend
at the waist over grim metal chairs—
black coffee and cigarettes—
the task of sobriety scrawled
on the blackboard of their souls.

Ask them a question and be prepared
for large slices of sincere, hard-fought
non sequiturs. Turn your head
from sunken eyes, the human cigarette
smoldering, limbo disguised as purgatory.

Pull up a chair. They don't
have a prayer—they have many.
What you have is a drink clouded
by smoke and desire. Memory swirls.
A song they once danced to,
dim smile crooked in drunk light.

Flash of crooked teeth and lust and illusionary
fancy footwork sidestepping hours
alone and what they will not discuss
while the sweet voices of someone else's
children rise above the fray of another
funeral or wedding or garage graduation party.

Look at the neatly printed signatures
on their checks. The strain
of the straight lines
to be understood.

Watching Another Drug Bust

outside the building across the street—
two young guys stiffly mute,
surrounded by the narco squad
in their bright orange t-shirts
joking around like jocks after a big win—
I press my hands against the glass.
I'd go over and pat their narco butts myself
if that did not expose me
to future reference.

The police, on my side at last
against the short guy with the green hat
and the fat guy with the limp
and the guns removed from their waistbands
and the black plastic bags full of product.

Beside me, my kids gawk out the window.
Just like on TV, my son says.
Show's over, I say.

◙

When we see the same guys out front
while we're waiting for the school bus
a week later
the kids say nothing. I yank weeds
from sidewalk cracks in gray dawn light.
Hoping for a rerun?
A commercial for the system?
I'm out of smart remarks,
my brave front slumping.
When the bus arrives, they ascend
and take their seats.

Eye contact is a disease.
Cash contaminated.
Future chalk outlines
smudged cartoons
blurred signatures
of what's acceptable
in a court of law. Laughable.

Okay, I've gone too far.
Okay, I've not gone far enough—
hat and limp open for business,
product available.

Morning sunshine—
gonna be a hot one, eh?
Eh? What you looking at?

I do a quick dance up the driveway.
Only God can describe it—
if he's got his eyes open
this early.

Boxing Toward the Promised Land

My friend who wrote *Keep your punch*
didn't himself. Wind 20–30 mph. Pine trees
across the street boogying in it—shake, rattle,
and roll. My friend and a shotgun in Pueblo.
He'd tried to start over, training to be a nurse,
but his hands shook when he gave shots,
fingers abuzz with heroin aftershocks.
The clouds roll in with a smeared menace.

No such thing as starting over. The uneven hammer-
ing of his ancient typewriter. Faint withering
of his scrawled name. His infrequent grin
once lit a forty-watt bulb for thirty seconds.
Keep your punch. I used his note as a bookmark
till I lost the book.

A soccer ball has escaped. Aided and abetted by wind.
It blows against a car tire. It spins out
and into traffic. You know the rest of that ball's
story. I almost wish I'd been more surprised
by the news. If *my* pills stop working, what kind
of dance will I be doing? Pine-tree boogie, rain
blowing in, the spilled ink of birds in a hurry.
Keep your punch. I make a fist. Two fists.

Curtains sway with a sudden disappearance.
A beating heart merges with footsteps
pounding up the stairs. Silence carries
its own venom and many false antidotes.
I once saw a statue of Cupid in a boxing pose.
I once saw a Rottweiler tear off a child's arm.
They sewed the arm back on, but Cupid went down
in the eighth round. Went down. Stayed down.

The Gravity of Math

My daughter counts how many people
will love her forever. She says *two*
(me and her mother). My son says *three*.
Does that mean you love me? she asks.
He's seven. She's six. The moon is nearly
full. Dreams are silent. I'm counting
how many slabs of gray stone I've leaned
against. He admits it, buckled in
behind me. I can't see back there.
The lights pour loosely onto the pavement
in front of us, spilling around the corner
toward home. *Feel my heart*, she says.
The world tilts. I lean into the turn.

Cosmetic

Last week my mother had eyebrows tattooed on.
She asks how they look. She's legally blind—
I could tell her anything.

It's been raining all day, shame's mad swirl
circling the house. No more cigarettes, coffee.
No more booze. *You've got to keep going*, I tell her.

I could be Annie in her cute red curls. You can
bet your bottom dollar. Pretty soon I'll be
tap-dancing on the coffee table, or up in my old room

crying. She's fingering the earphones of her books-
on-tape machine. She's been saving up things
to tell me. She ticks them off like the giant

grocery list graffitied to her fridge. I've collected
scraps of her old handwriting, the graceful swirls

of confidence. 75 years of good vision. She's rounding
everything off into simple shapes. I'm staring

at the all-weather eyebrows. A cartoon looking
for the punch line. I run my finger over them.

She startles, then relaxes. *It made her sneeze*,
my father offers up from the kitchen

where he's spending a lot more time. *Your father
stopped saying 'Bless you' pretty fast.*

Good. Great. Fantastic. Exquisite. The eyebrows
to top all eyebrows. The king and queen of eyebrow.

Listen to the rain, she says.
Just listen to it coming down.

Listening to "96 Tears" by ? and the Mysterians While Looking Down from My Third-Floor Window at a Kid Crossing the Panther Hollow Bridge

Snow kicks up the volume.
Okay, squint and push yourself
past the two gilded cats guarding
the empty bridge. Lean into
the wind like an old friend
who's going to hold up
your drunken ass. Late,
and even the traffic whine
is stilled. Listen up,
sucker. The System
is just a steamroller
moonbeam, and The Man
is an aging seven-footer
who can still block your
shots. And you're done
growing, for sure. It'd
be easy to lean over the rail
and drop into a small item
at the bottom of the page,
cause unknown.
I sit awake and warm
high above you. You
could have an entirely different
story ready if stopped.
My wife and children
sleep softly beneath me,
but I had a blue jacket
like that once.

Elegy for the Nasty Neighbor

across the street who died at last. I've already
forgiven myself the relief—that fast,

that mean. Her last words to me,
a complaint about red mulch

I'd spread on the traffic island I maintain
voluntarily. *Too red*, she screeched.

It'll fade, but I said nothing. She lived
alone with her daughter, who sits on the porch

at this moment, flipping through, what?
Condolence cards from the senior center?

Bills? The paperwork of the dead? First, the yappy
little dog, now the old lady. She knows she's next.

The mulch matches exactly the color
of their shingles. Still doesn't keep the weeds down

as claimed. I'm out on hands and knees, not praying.
I'm digging, and the daughter says something about working

the earth bringing you closer to God. She wouldn't know God
if he broke off her side-view mirror and turned it into a set

of dazzling silver teeth. I wouldn't know God if he turned my mulch
into gold nuggets. But we're thinking about him, wondering,

if he's a real dude, what he's doing with the old bitch about now.
The daughter, my age, has never pulled one weed on our communal

island. They complained when I dug up what they claimed were flowers.
When my wife nearly died in a car accident on the street, they stayed
	inside,

then came out later to tell the cops it was her fault. Helpless
with pettiness, I cannot dig up all of the roots. Grudges.

Can't live with 'em, can't live without 'em.
I shake the daughter's hand and give her my condolences.

She wants to talk about who broke off her mirror.
Condolences come cheap. Gray sky, fifth of July,

thick wet sand we're breathing here in Pittsburgh,
far from any beach. I'm trying to steer my urban canoe

back to where I'm the Good Guy. Charity begins with cheap trinkets
and ends in insincere exchanges. Sale on condolences.

It's finally raining now, or is God spitting on me? Some weeds—
to get the roots, you'd have to dig all the way to hell. Or Red China.

They both cuss(ed) like lost sailors, stranded far from their ships
with a broken compass and a yippy dog. They sounded like yippy dogs

together on their porch, nipping at each other. And if I sound
like all bark and no bite, it's true.

I miss Red China, the mysterious hatred that was expected.
Our street so gray I thought a little red might help.

A horn beeps, and we both turn. Just another impatient drug buyer
in front of the building next door. I own a wide array

of weed diggers, but not one gun. I held her hand briefly.
Sorry about your mother. The queen is dead.

Long live the queen's nasty daughter.
The reckless spreading of fourteen bags of red mulch

across the long, thin island, around the trees and bushes,
filled me with deep, profound joy and menace,

ripping open the bulky plastic bags like I was tearing
apart my chest, letting it all spill out.

It's just China now. That whole Red thing—
well, you'll have to read the book on that.

I want Blue Canada and Orange Mexico
and Purple Haze and Green Green Rocky Road.

Her name was Mrs. Kearns, and that's all anybody
called her. Okay, I sometimes called her The Mouth,

her voice injecting shrill bile into my veins.
They had two identical dogs, both named Trixie.

Yappy, and both dead. The red roof, the red mulch,
the Bouquet Avenue blues. Life is toxic. I miss her already,

the claws of her hands, the bitter gnarl around the lousy cards
she insisted on bluffing with. You can call me Neighbor Jim

though nobody does. The dye from the mulch
rubbed off onto her daughter's hand when I shook it.

Shook on whatever makes us both tremble.
Rain bounces off my bucket, my tools. Weeds

already rising from the dead. God has it in for me
just like everybody else, and that much is true.

Life is decorative. The mulch is guaranteed
to keep its color for six months. Then perhaps

it explodes. Some day maybe we'll all meet in Red China
to sort it all out. It'll fade, I could've said,

but I said nothing.

Souvenir

When he was my age, my father took
a deliberate demotion. The chubby ball boy
at the Pirates game last Sunday
handed my son a foul ball.

We'd never sat in the first row before.
When I was ten, a large man leaned over
to grab a ball tossed by Frank Robinson
right out of my cupped hands. He held it proudly aloft.

My father took his demotion after burying
two co-workers. He didn't talk about it then
or now. He took me to my first game
as a communion gift—Tiger Stadium's

impossibly green grass, Harmon Killebrew
smacking one out for the Twins.
He worked so many hours that even now
I can't stop counting. Last month, he revealed

that he told neighbors he was growing
Japanese Dwarf Grass to explain our stunted lawn.
My father telling a joke—I take time imagining
that. My brothers and I stomped that grass

while he was working. We have no yard here,
and our stadium has fake grass. They call it turf
to make it sound better. Even Harmon Killebrew
looked pretty small from the upper deck.

My first communion—donuts on the ping-pong
table, then Harmon. He hit 573 career homers.
I don't have to look it up. My father worked
at Ford's. Henry Ford's. That apostrophe

means everything in Detroit.

My father asked for a demotion.
A star pitcher in high school,
he knotted his arm with early curves.
Clippings in a cigar box.

A rich friend gave me the good seats.
I remembered to tip the usher. I am wanting
a demotion. My son likes home runs, the ball's
disappearance. Other boys held out their mitts,
but the ball boy picked out my timid son.

After the game, I waited under the stands,
but Robinson would not sign my scorebook.
What ball? he griped, as I stalked him
down the dark corridor to the team bus.

I stood waiting hours for my own bus home
on the wrong side of the street—
sometimes you just have to smile
that sad little smile that says,

I'll take my lumps, okay. I'll take my demotion,
okay. I want a demotion so I can breathe
a little deeper without the sharp jabs.
So I can take extra batting practice.

I love green grass but not the taming of lawns.
My father throws a great knuckler even now.
I still can't catch it. I chased his pitches
over bumpy sidewalks, then threw the ball back

to him high and far. We didn't play much catch—
I hope this doesn't sound whiny, like if we'd just played
a little more, the world would be a better place. Memories
are like that. High and far.

Albert Pujols hit a three-run homer for the Cards.
On pace to break a lot of records. If he stays healthy.
If he doesn't retire early. We've left our mitts out
in the rain once already, my son and I.

I hope the company lets me go back to my old job.
All grass is artificial. I love my father with his battered suitcase
of the unspoken. I love my son with his scuffed prize.
I once saw Frank Howard hit one over the roof

at Tiger Stadium. That same day, my friend Billy Bowen
won a free ham in the lucky number scorebook drawing.
I never saw that ball come down. It just disappeared,
white ball against white sky, memory against time.

Acknowledgments

Special thanks to the editors of the following publications where these poems first appeared:

The American Voice in Poetry: The Legacy of Whitman, Williams, and Ginsberg: "Company Men";
Caffeine Destiny: "One Arm Raised";
Cerise Press: "The Geography of Detroit";
Cimarron Review: "Hit and Run," "Love Poem with Pesticide";
Connotation Press: "Those of Us Without AC";
Conte: "Riding the Bench";
Court Green: "45 RPM: Side A/Side B";
Detroit Stories: "Good Reception," "Souvenir";
The Fourth River: "Watching Another Drug Bust";
Gargoyle: "Foundation";
The Georgia Review: "The Family Price";
The Gettysburg Review: "Cosmetic," "Record Accumulation";
Gigantic Sequins: "The Laying on of Hands";
Green Mountains Review: "The Religious Significance of the Super Ball";
Harpur Palate: "Birth Marks";
Hotel Amerika: "Elegy for the Nasty Neighbor";
The Indiana Review: "Recreational Trail";
Iron Horse Literary Review: "Feed Corn";
Lake Effect: "Exterior with Quiet";
The Literary Review: "Church Reform";
Paddlefish: "Approaching and Passing an Epiphany";
Pleiades: "Taking the Leap";
poetrymagazine.com: "Treaty";
Rattle: "The Dark Miracle," "Lip Gloss, Belgium";
Riverwind: "Final/Not Final";
The Same: "The Worn Knees and Elbows of My Alcoholic Uncles";
Smartish Pace: "I Dreamt I Wrote a Poem About Jazz";
Subtropics: "One Word";
Sugar House Review: "On Tears";

The Sycamore Review: "My Two Aunts," "Poetica No Apologia Arte Kumbaya";

TriQuarterly: "Listening to '96 Tears' by ? and the Mysterians While Looking Down from My Third-Floor Window at a Kid Crossing the Panther Hollow Bridge";

Water-Stone: "The Gravity of Math";

Willow Springs: "MegaEverything";

Zone 3: "Making a Case for the Letter".

"Boxing Toward the Promised Land" and "Church Reform" appeared in the chapbook, *Now Showing*, ahadada press, 2006.

"The Dark Miracle" is for Demetria Martinez.
"Boxing Toward the Promised Land" is for Paul Dilsaver.

About the Author

Jim Daniels is the author of fourteen collections of poetry, four collections of fiction, and three produced screenplays. He has received the Brittingham Prize for Poetry, the Tillie Olsen Prize, the Blue Lynx Poetry Prize, two fellowships from the National Endowment for the Arts, and two from the Pennsylvania Council on the Arts. His poems have appeared in the *Pushcart Prize* and *Best American Poetry* anthologies, and his poem "Factory Love" is displayed on the roof of a race car. At Carnegie Mellon University, he is the Thomas Stockham Baker Professor of English. A native of Detroit, Daniels lives with his family in Pittsburgh near the boyhood homes of Andy Warhol and Dan Marino.

BOA Editions, Ltd.
American Poets Continuum Series

Colophon

BOA Editions, Ltd., a not-for-profit publisher of poetry and other literary works, fosters readership and appreciation of contemporary literature. By identifying, cultivating, and publishing both new and established poets and selecting authors of unique literary talent, BOA brings high-quality literature to the public. Support for this effort comes from the sale of its publications, grant funding, and private donations.

The publication of this book is made possible, in part,
by the special support of the following individuals:

Anonymous
Nin Andrews
Bernadette Catalana
Anne Germanacos
Robert L. Giron
X. J. & Dorothy M. Kennedy
Laurie Kutchins
Peter & Phyllis Makuck
Daniel Meyers, *in honor of Boo Poulin*
Boo Poulin
Cindy W. Rogers
Steven O. Russell & Phyllis Rifkin-Russell
Michael Waters & Mihaela Moscaliuc